A Mother is a Story

A Celebration of Motherhood

By Samantha Hahn

ABRAMS, NEW YORK

DEDICATION

———————————

*For Henry and Vivian. No words ever written are powerful
enough to convey my love for you.*

*And to Every Mother Counts, an organization dedicated
to making pregnancy and childbirth safe for every mother.
For more information, please visit: www.everymothercounts.org.*

INTRODUCTION

If I could distill the feeling in my heart when I first looked at my children, each time I smelled them or felt the softness of their skin and the warmth of their bodies, I would bottle it against the days I both dread and feverishly work toward, when they need me in their hearts but are strong enough to stand apart.

Becoming a mother gives you insight into the mind of your own mother; it allows you to see from her perspective for the first time and deepens the bond you share. The world looks different, and you are somehow even more grounded in it, more connected than ever before.

Creating this book, I wanted to see if it was possible to portray this shared experience of motherhood in all its glorious, messy beauty. I've found that each quote resonates at different moments, as different aspects of this incredible journey come to pass. To paraphrase Meghan O'Rourke, a mother is a story, and nothing can prepare you for the constant whirlwind of emotions, often simultaneous and conflicting. Deeply in love and deeply exhausted, exasperated and proud, worried and blissful—these feelings form their own special harmony and become the story of motherhood.

I hope these words and illustrations strike a chord with you. I hope you recognize yourself, your children, your mother, and the love that passes between you all in these pages.

"A mother is a story with no beginning."

—MEGHAN O'ROURKE

"A Mother is always the Beginning. She is how things begin."

—AMY TAN

"Perhaps if
we saw what was ahead of us,
and glimpsed the crimes,
follies, and misfortunes
that would befall us later on,
we would all stay
in our mother's wombs,
and then there would be
nobody in the world but
a great number
of very fat,
very irritated
women."

—LEMONY SNICKET

"THERE IS A WONDROUS CURIOSITY IN EVERY YOUNG MOTHER.

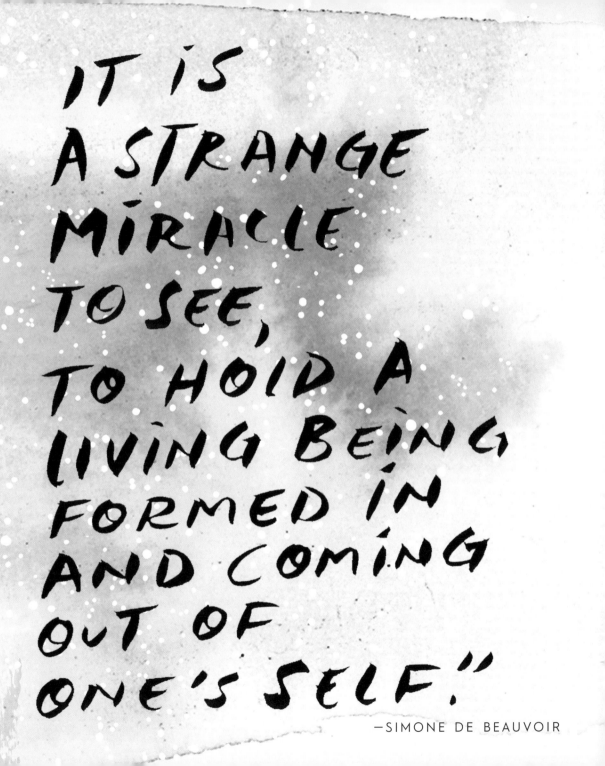

IT IS A STRANGE MIRACLE TO SEE, TO HOLD A LIVING BEING FORMED IN AND COMING OUT OF ONE'S SELF."

—SIMONE DE BEAUVOIR

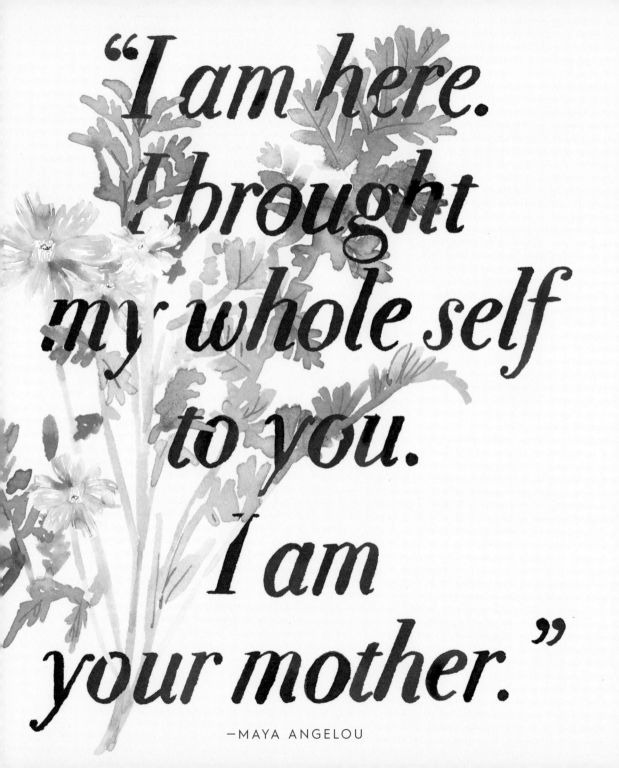

"I am here. I brought my whole self to you. I am your mother."

—MAYA ANGELOU

"Just as there is no warning for childbirth, there is no preparation for the sight of a first child.... There should be a song for women to sing at this moment, or a prayer to recite. But perhaps there is none because there are no words strong enough to name that moment."

—ANITA DIAMANT

"A FEW DAYS AFTER
WE CAME HOME
FROM THE HOSPITAL,
I SENT A LETTER
TO A FRIEND,
INCLUDING A PHOTO
OF MY SON AND
SOME FIRST
IMPRESSIONS
OF FATHERHOOD.

HE RESPONDED, simply,
'EVERYTHING IS
POSSIBLE AGAIN.'
IT WAS THE PERFECT THING TO
WRITE, BECAUSE THAT WAS EXACTLY
HOW IT FELT."

—JONATHAN SAFRAN FOER

"We never know the love of a parent till we become parents ourselves."

—HENRY WARD BEECHER

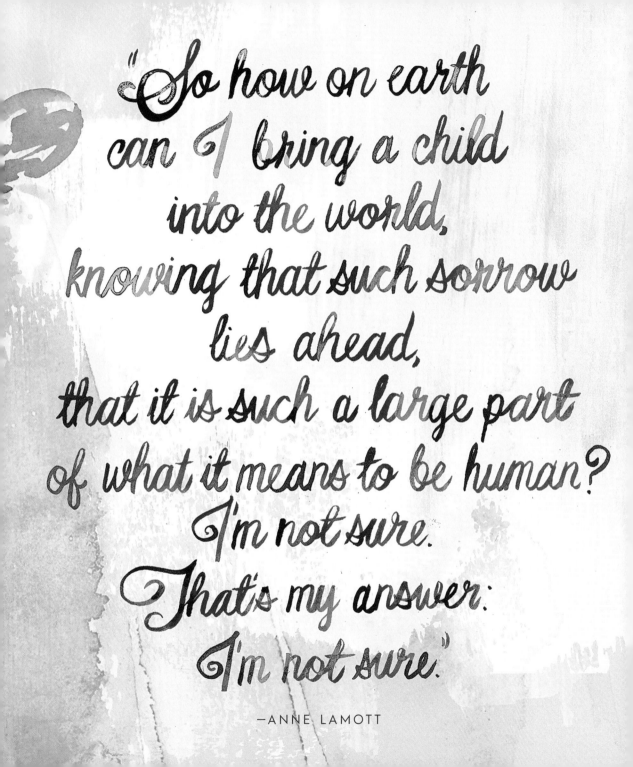

"So how on earth can I bring a child into the world, knowing that such sorrow lies ahead, that it is such a large part of what it means to be human? I'm not sure. That's my answer: I'm not sure."

—ANNE LAMOTT

"'Truly it is not easy
to bring up a family,'
sighs Babar.
'But how nice the babies are!
I wouldn't know how to get
along without them any more.'"

—JEAN DE BRUNHOFF

"The human
heart
was not designed
to beat
outside
the human body
and yet,

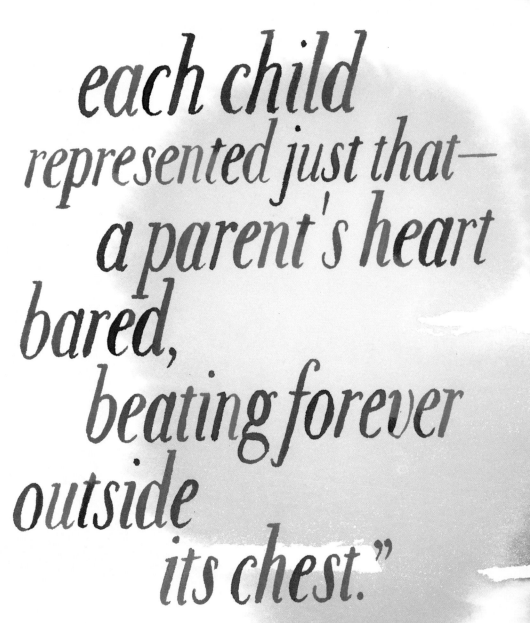

each child represented just that—a parent's heart bared, beating forever outside its chest."

—DEBRA GINSBERG

"A mother's heart is always with her children."

—PROVERB

"A Mother's love for her child is like nothing else in the world. It knows no law, no pity, it dares all things and crushes down remorselessly all that stands in its path."

—AGATHA CHRISTIE

"A mother's arms are made of tenderness and children sleep soundly in them."

—VICTOR HUGO

"Can anything harm us, mother, after the night-lights are lit?"

'Nothing, precious,' she said; 'they are the eyes a mother leaves behind her to guard her children.'"

—J. M. BARRIE

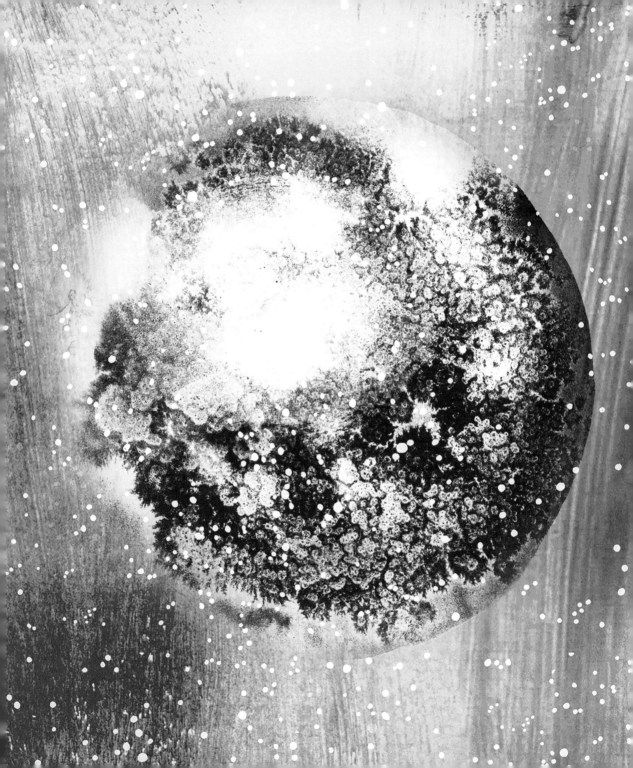

"All of a sudden, the moon and I were the best of friends. The nights were long and we were awake, walking in circles around the house, rocking the baby back to sleep."

—EMMA STRAUB

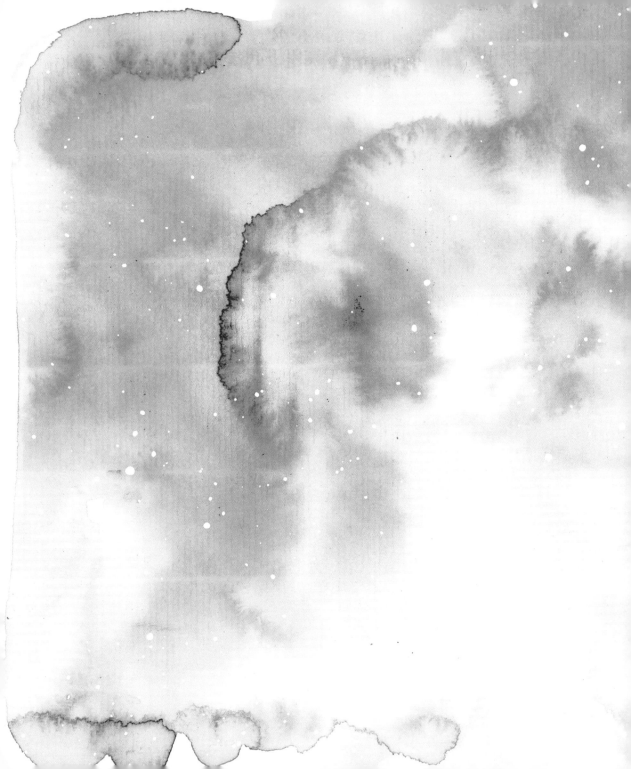

"Over my slumbers your loving watch keep;
– Rock me to sleep, mother
– rock me to sleep."

—ELIZABETH AKERS ALLEN

"The heart
of a mother
is a deep abyss
at the bottom
of which
you will always
find forgiveness."

—HONORÉ DE BALZAC

"I never had a mother. I suppose a mother is one

to whom
you hurry
when you
are
troubled."

—EMILY DICKINSON

"Motherhood is at its best when the tender chords of sympathy have been touched."

—PAUL HARRIS

"I think that I see something deeper, more infinite, more eternal than the ocean in the expression of the eyes of a little baby when it wakes in the morning and coos or laughs because it sees the sun shining on its cradle."

—VINCENT VAN GOGH

"A mother knows what her child's gone through, even if she didn't see it herself."

—PRAMOEDYA ANANTA TOER

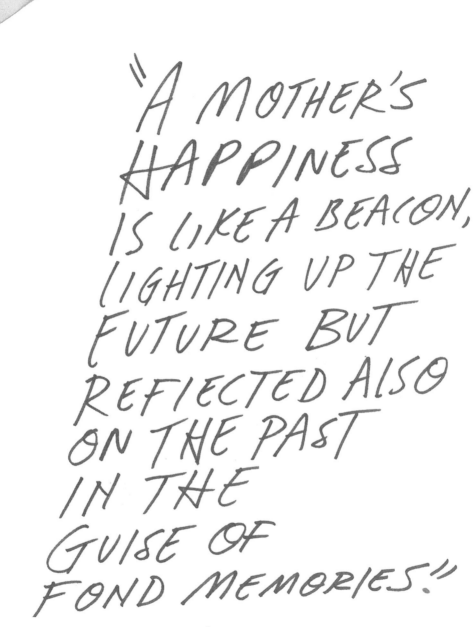

"A MOTHER'S HAPPINESS IS LIKE A BEACON, LIGHTING UP THE FUTURE BUT REFLECTED ALSO ON THE PAST IN THE GUISE OF FOND MEMORIES."

—HONORÉ DE BALZAC

"When you become a mom, you get to believe in *magic* again."

—ATHENA CALDERONE

"The goodness
of the mother
is written
is written

in the gaiety
of the child"

—VICTOR HUGO

"When your children arrive, the best you can hope for is that they break open everything about you.

Your mind floods
with oxygen.
Your heart
becomes a room
with wide-open windows.
You laugh hard
every day."

—AMY POEHLER

my

biness."

—NATHANIEL HAWTHORNE

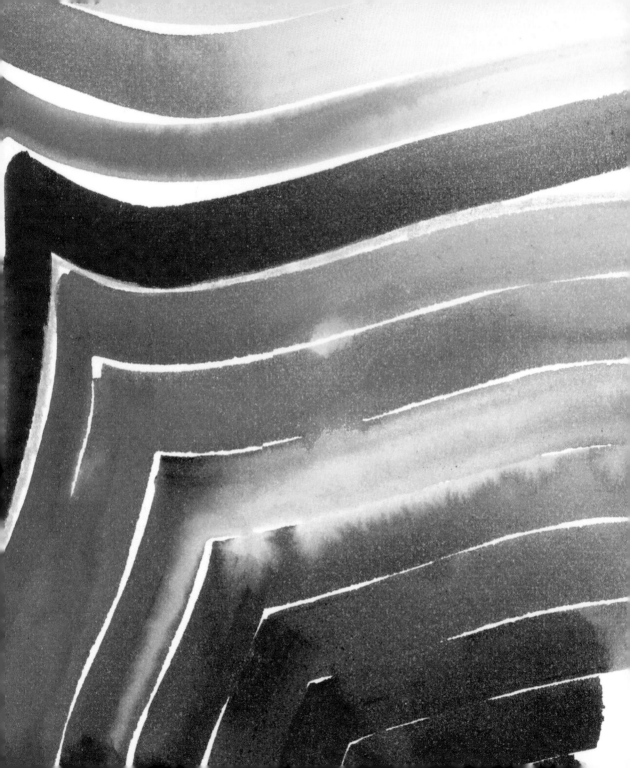

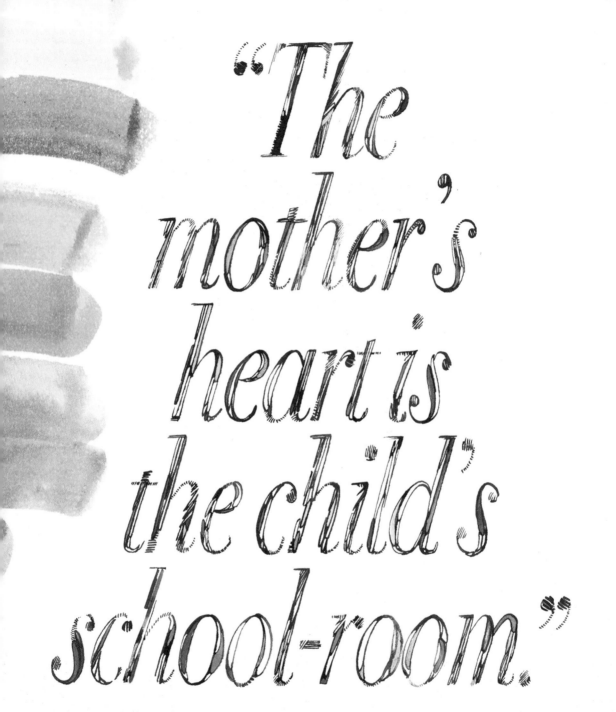

"The mother's heart is the child's school-room."

—HENRY WARD BEECHER

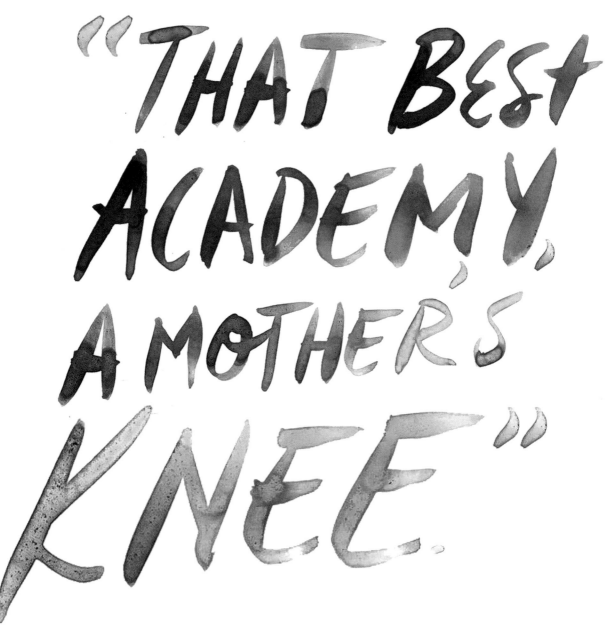

"THAT BEST ACADEMY, A MOTHER'S KNEE"

—JAMES RUSSELL LOWELL

"What the child says, he has heard at home."

—AFRICAN PROVERB

"I am sure that if the mothers of various nations could meet, there would be no more wars..."

—E. M. FORSTER

"When I am not paying attention to my children, they appear to desperately need it. When I am giving them my full attention, they seem just as happy to play by themselves. It is as though they need to be certain of my attention in order to play their own games and ignore me." —SARAH RUHL

"Mother says as th'
two worst things as can
happen to a child is
never to have his own way—
or always to have it.
She doesn't know which
is th' worst."

—FRANCES HODGSON BURNETT

"The best
way to keep
children
at home
is to
make

the home
atmosphere
pleasant—
and let the
air out of
the tires. "

—DOROTHY PARKER

"If evolution really works, how come mothers only have two hands?"

—MILTON BERLE

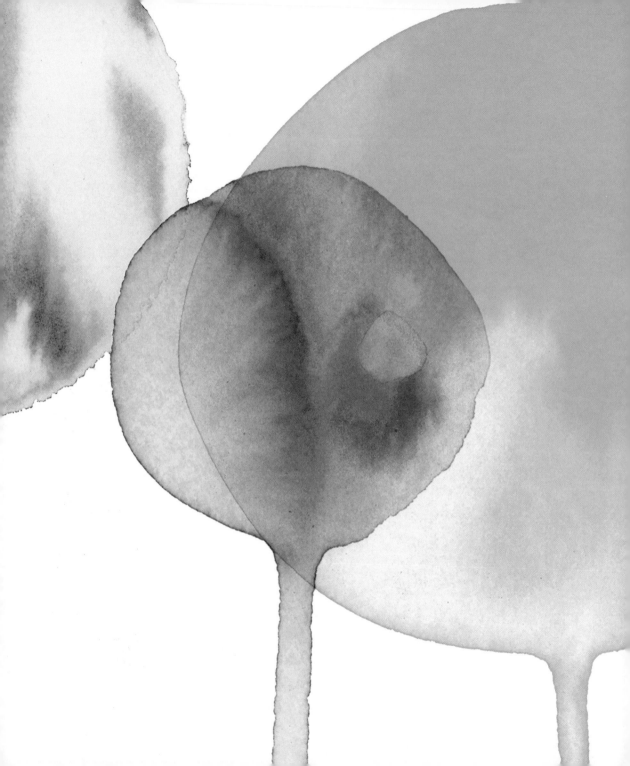

"My mother had a good deal of trouble with me, but I think she enjoyed it."

—MARK TWAIN

"The love of a mother is never exhausted; it never changes, it never tires."

—WASHINGTON IRVING

"If you knew how great is a mother's love you would have no fear."

—J. M. BARRIE

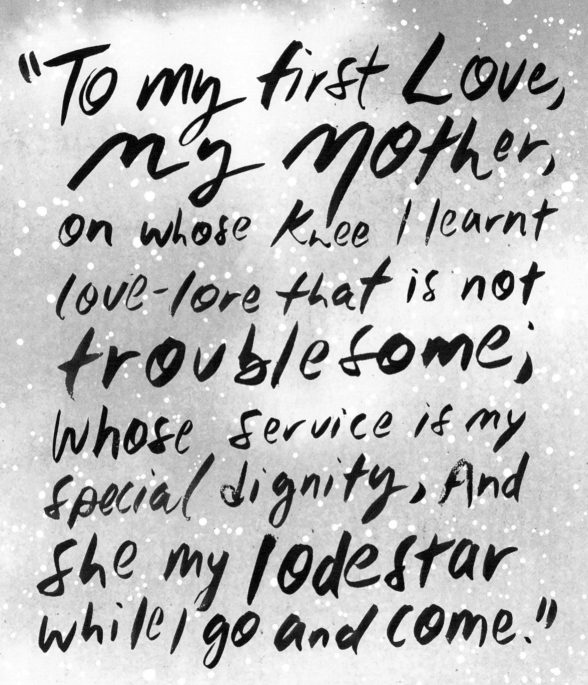

"To my first Love, my mother, on whose knee I learnt love-lore that is not troublesome; whose service is my special dignity, And she my lodestar while I go and come."

—CHRISTINA ROSSETTI

"A mother is

bu

make

not a person
to lean on
a person to
leaning
unnecessary. "

—DOROTHY CANFIELD FISHER

"All that I am or ever hope to be, I owe to my angel mother."

—ABRAHAM LINCOLN

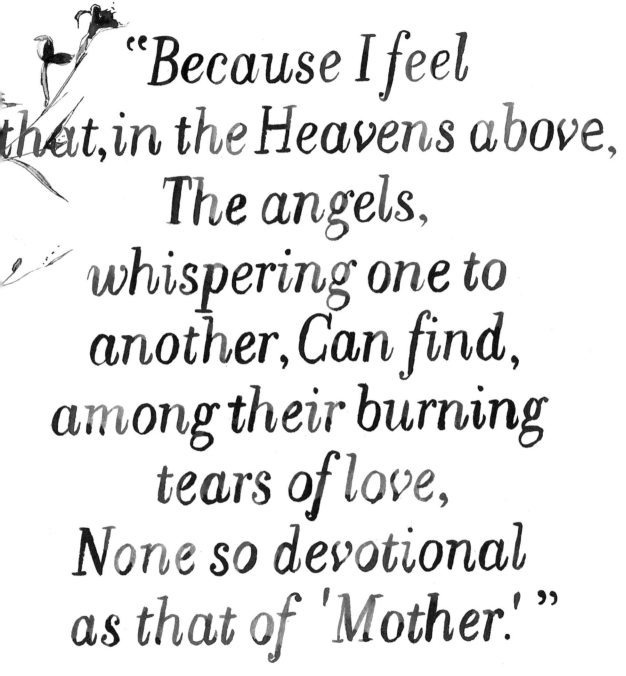

"Because I feel
that, in the Heavens above,
The angels,
whispering one to
another, Can find,
among their burning
tears of love,
None so devotional
as that of 'Mother.'"

—EDGAR ALLAN POE

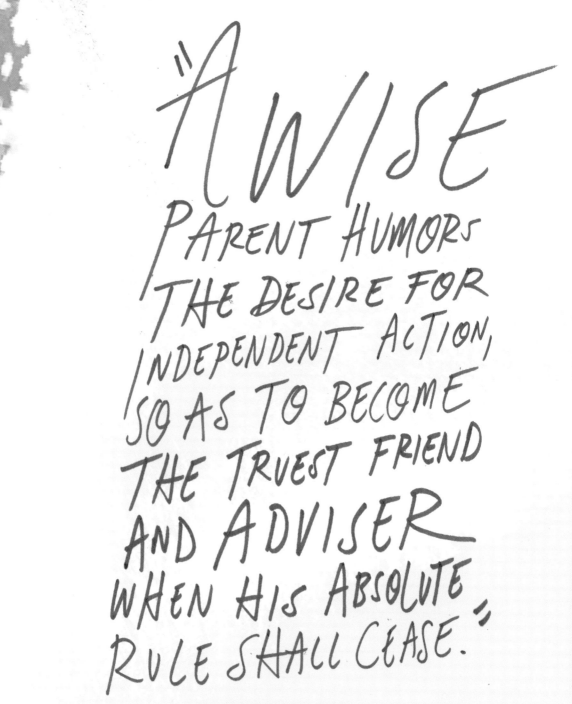

"A WISE PARENT HUMORS THE DESIRE FOR INDEPENDENT ACTION, SO AS TO BECOME THE TRUEST FRIEND AND ADVISER WHEN HIS ABSOLUTE RULE SHALL CEASE."

—ELIZABETH GASKELL

"Parents are programmed to want the best for their kids, regardless of what they get in return."

—JONATHAN FRANZEN

"The danger in motherhood. You relive your early self, through the eyes of your own Mother."

—JOYCE CAROL OATES

"I like to think of motherhood as a great big adventure. You set off on a journey, you don't really know how to navigate things, and you don't know exactly where you're going or how you're going to get there."

—CYNTHIA ROWLEY

"This moment right here
is the best it's ever been.
Every moment has been
the best it's ever been.
I have an entire lifetime
of the best it's ever beens
to come, and oh boy
do I look forward to it."

—NATALIE HOLBROOK

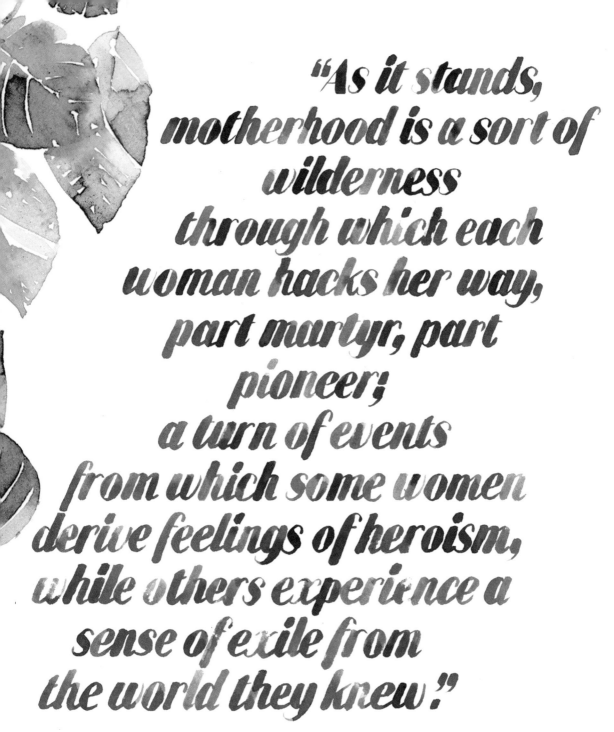

"As it stands, motherhood is a sort of wilderness through which each woman hacks her way, part martyr, part pioneer; a turn of events from which some women derive feelings of heroism, while others experience a sense of exile from the world they knew."

—RACHEL CUSK

"OH WHAT A POWER IS MOTHERHOOD"

—EURIPIDES

"WE ARE BORN OF LOVE; LOVE IS OUR MOTHER."

—RUMI

"No langua

can express

and beauty,

and

qe the power, and heroism, majesty of a mother's love."

—EDWIN HUBBELL CHAPIN

ACKNOWLEDGMENTS

Thank you to my mom, Marika; my mother-in-law, Susan;
Nana Sally; and aunts Lizzie, Lisa, Irene, and Myrna for showing me
what a mother is.

Thank you to Dave, my loving husband; the way you parent inspires me.

Thank you to my agent, Alison Fargis, and editors Camaren and Karrie,
as well as everyone at Abrams.

Thank you to Charlotte Strick and Hana Nakamura.

Also, thanks to all my mama friends, whose beautiful families inspired
many of the images on these pages, especially: Erin Jang, Abby Low,
Randi Brookman Harris, Liz Libre, Linsey Laidlaw, Violet Gaynor,
and Elizabeth Antonia.

CREDITS

EDITORS: Camaren Subhiyah and Karrie Witkin
PRODUCTION MANAGER: True Sims

Library of Congress Control Number: 2015946902

ISBN: 978-1-4197-2015-4

Illustrations copyright © 2016 Samantha Hahn

Printed and bound in China
10 9 8 7 6 5 4 3 2 1

Abrams books are available at special discounts when
purchased in quantity for premiums and promotions as
well as fundraising or educational use. Special editions
 can also be created to specification. For details, contact
specialsales@abramsbooks.com or the address below.

THE ART OF BOOKS SINCE 1949
115 West 18th Street
New York, NY 10011
www.abramsbooks.com